MY SACRAMENT IN VERSE

My First Efforts in the Art of Writing Prose

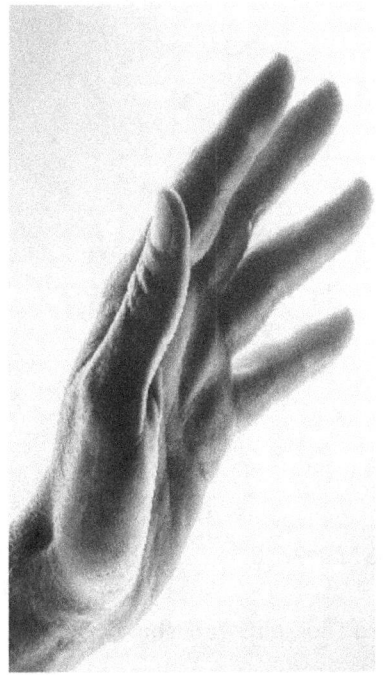

DOUGLAS J. ESCHER

All Scripture quotations are taken from the Holy Bible, New International Version®, NIV®. Copyright © 1973, 1978, 1984, 2011 by Biblica, Inc.™ Used by permission of Zondervan. All rights reserved worldwide. www.zondervan.com. The "NIV" and "New International Version" are trademarks registered in the United States Patent and Trademark Office by Biblica, Inc.™

My Sacrament in Verse
Copyright © 2025 by Douglas J. Escher
ISBN: 978-1-685730-75-8

Published by Word and Spirit Publishing
P.O. Box 701403
Tulsa, Oklahoma 74170
wordandspiritpublishing.com

Printed in the United States of America. All rights reserved under International Copyright Law. Content and/or cover may not be reproduced in whole or in part in any form without the expressed written consent of the Publisher.

DEDICATION

My Sacrament in Verse is dedicated to two lifetime friends: Phil and Marge Ouimette. They provided the opportunity for me to move to Rochester, New York. They hoped that their mentally wounded soldier and friend could make a new start. After fifty-one years here in Rochester, that new life is being lived with gratitude and thanks. I have been blessed beyond belief.

Thank you, Phil and Marge, and all of your family! May God continue to bless you, as He has blessed me.

—Douglas J. Escher

ACKNOWLEDGMENTS

Jenny Ertel made this book come alive! She shared her edits, image selection, and layout for each story. Even more worthy was her patience with me. She simply was and is a true blessing. Thank you, Jenny, for making this dream a reality. God bless you!

CONTENTS

Preface ... ix

My Home
Up and at 'Em ... 2
Welcome ... 3
Perfect Excuse ... 4

Me
Magic Mind ... 7
Wishing Well ... 9
Wishes ... 11

Today
Rise Anew ... 14
Search ... 16
Bad Luck Duck ... 18
Signs of Winter ... 20
Today ... 21

On My Mind
Crippled Me ... 25
Strangers ... 27
Money ... 29
"Basic War" ... 30
Working ... 33
Too Much and Not Enough ... 35
Helping ... 37

What I've Learned So Far
The Journey   41
Faith and Doubt   42
Encouragement   43

This I Know
Visions   46
A Drop of Love   47
Time Left   50

Make Ready
State of Soul   53

PREFACE

This is a photograph of the author, Doug Escher, when he was a Huey helicopter crew member in the Vietnam War. In 1970, upon his return home, at the age of twenty-one, he, like so many other Vietnam veterans, had struggles adjusting to his new life back home as a civilian.

He moved from Oneonta, New York, to Rochester, New York, in 1973, in hopes of a more successful restart to his life. His new job was an entry-level position that barely provided a living wage, and he was left with more time than money to spend. During that time, between 1973 and 1975, Doug suddenly found a calling to write prose, and this book is the outcome of those efforts.

Remarkably, in August 2023, he awoke one day to a heavily flooded basement, the result of which was a reunion with his writings from forty-eight to fifty years past. After reviewing his prose, others suggested to him it was time to publish them in a book.

He desires that you, the reader, would relax and read these pages one by one, in the hopes of discovering some insight along with enjoyment!

Therefore, if anyone is in Christ, the new creation has come. The old has gone, the new is here! All this is from God.
—2 Corinthians 5:17–18

My Home

Up and at 'Em

Get up and get at 'em.
Another day of work,
thanks to Eve and Adam.

Welcome

Welcome to our happy home,
And thanks to you, we're not alone.

Just be relaxed and be yourself.
Let us tend to everything else.

But if a helping hand is required,
Look out, neighbor, you've just been hired.

Perfect Excuse

Excuse this house if it appears to be a mess.
That's what happens when children live in your nest.

Me

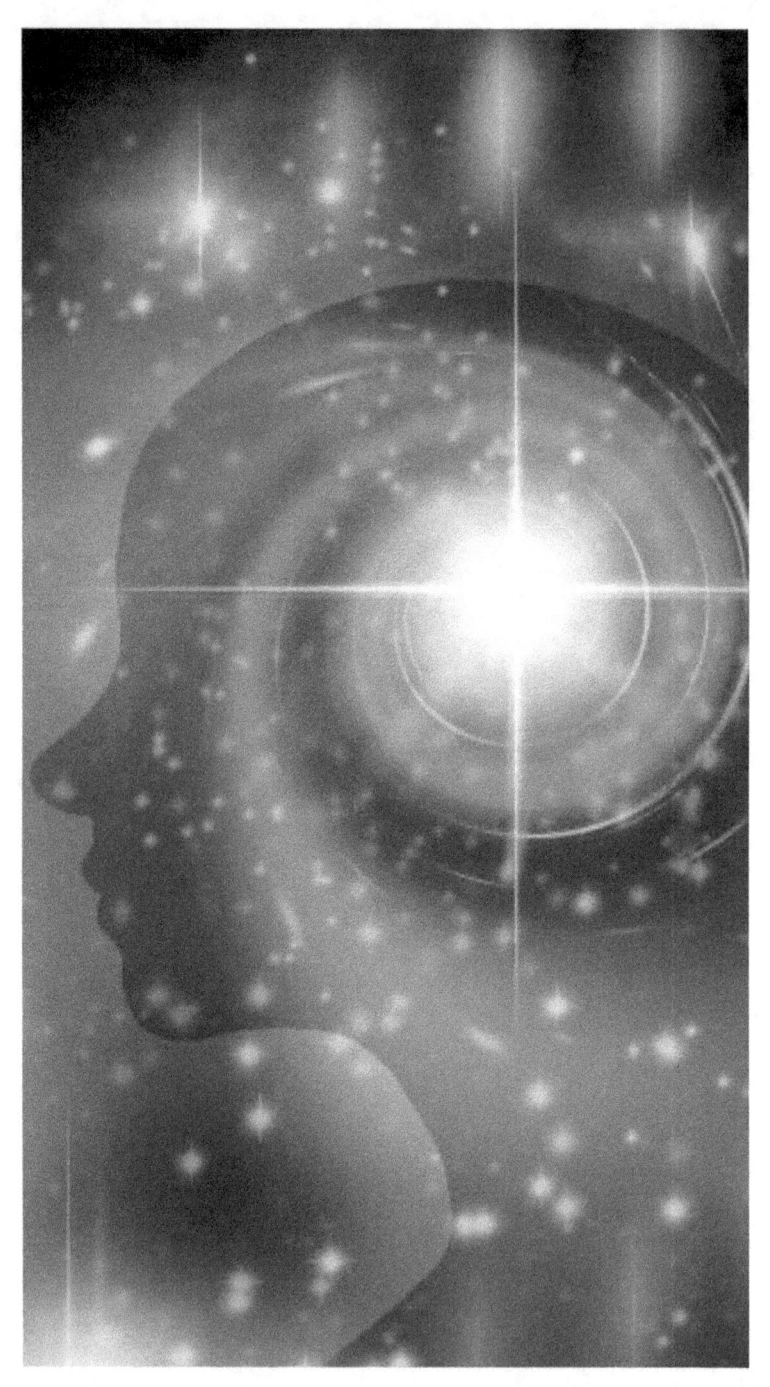

Magic Mind

What magic lies buried in the human mind?
It's hard to believe I have one, and it's all mine.

"Brain" is its given name,
And few have used it, but those who have, have reached a height called fame.

Everyone is given one to use;
And what you don't use, you simply lose.
If you haven't used yours, you must agree,
It would be as easy as can be.

Don't feel bad
If you haven't used what you have,
But do feel poor
If you refuse to use it anymore.

It can do anything you name,
But there appear to be rules to its game.
That only seems right, for without them, it just wouldn't be fair.

History will show there's no magic at all,
Mostly hard work, desire, and faith above all.

So play by the rules,
And it's impossible to lose.
Most of all, keep your faith, and the magic will not be an illustion.
The day will come when you'll say, "I did it I won."

Wishing Well

Make a wish at the wishing well.
Wishes are the only dreams it has to sell.

The price of a wish is only a mere copper penny.
For the wish granter says that is more than plenty.
The wish granter cannot be bribed
By the falseness money hides.

Just stand at the well and find
That special wish, and make it known deep inside.
Then toss your copper penny and your
Wish the granter will discover.

Now, if you have never made a wish at a wishing well,
Let me remind you it has your dream it wishes to sell.

Wishes

I wished I could be an artist and paint a tree.
I wished I could be a fisherman who fishes the clear blue sea.

I wished I could be an actor and have a leading role.
I wished I could be an athlete and catch or throw like Broadway Joe.

I wished I could be an astronaut and fly to the moon.
I wished I could be a character in a Walt Disney cartoon.

I wished I could be a cowboy and blaze the trails out west.
I wished I could be an executive and sit behind a big desk.

I've wished so many things, for they all seemed worthy of something to be,
But then someone said they made a wish—and they wished they could be like me!

Well, I was flattered, but my mind quickly scattered, to think someone would want my worries, my problems, and all those different things that make up me;
I didn't feel I was worthy of someone to be.

I quickly took all my wishes of things I wanted to be,
And I decided, *I'm just going to be me.*
Keep my own worries and problems, and just take the time to solve them. I'll be what I am going to be—
And that's just me.

Today

Rise Anew

Rise anew and get to your rested feet.
There's a new day to greet.
Don't delay;
Here is today, and yesterday's problems have now passed away.
Yesterday's victories will guide your way.

Search

Search for the greener valley, the wise man told,
But since then, I have grown quite old.

So off to the greener valley I went,
In trust I would find life greener yet.

Finally, the greener valley I sought I did find, but it was strange what I finally saw.
My greener valley was full of straw.

Whey my greener valley was full of straw was hard for me to understand.
The I recalled, I was merely a mortal man.
So I looked again, and what I saw
Was more than a valley of straw,
But there lay the greenest valley of all.

Now I am in my wisest years, for my experience has taught me well.
So now I say, search for the greener valley, and if you see it is full of straw,
You may also see the greenest valley of all.

Bad Luck Duck

I saw one duck flying freely through the air.
I saw hunters on the ground, it seemed, everywhere.

As the single duck flew over the hunters galore,
They opened fire from their camouflaged shore.

The duck seemed slightly alarmed at the shots he heard.
He looked more curious, wondering why so many shots at one small bird.

The duck was terminated in his flight
As he fell from his traveling height.

As he lay still in his watery grave,
The hunters sent out their dogs to retrieve what someone's bullet gave.

Now, I'm just wondering what so many will do with one small bird.
Maybe they were down on their luck and one duck was trophy enough for the day.
I remember I sat there the rest of the day, and no more ducks flew their way.

Signs of Winter

The flowers have grown old,
And Old Man Winter says it's time to ready for snow.

The leaves have lost all their freshly colored green,
And their new colors make for a beautiful autumn scene.

Our four-legged neighbors are starting to grow more hair,
For Mother Nature says, "There will soon be a chill in the air."

The bears are starting to yawn,
For the warmer weather is almost gone.

The birds are leaving for the south.
Not much food will be found on the winter's frozen ground, but in the south they will find food enough for each and every mouth.

All the bugs and pests are quietly laid to rest.
Many are happy to say goodbye to that bunch of frustrating guests.

Yes, winder does not leap into the air.
Mother Nature gives adequate signs and time to prepare.

Let's get ready for the cold we will share.
Haven't you often wished you were the bear?

Today

The new day is over, as the freshest tomorrow is in the awaiting wake,
As I can now sit back and wonder what it is of today that I myself did make.

Did I do enough to pay the debt of my daily dues?
How many battles did I win, and how many did I lose?
How many new paths did I walk, and how many old ones did I cruise?
What is it about today that can tell me, "Today I won and did not lose"?

On My Mind

Crippled Me

I used to laugh at the crippled ones,
Feeling they were misfits—just meant for fun.

I knew I was far superior for I had all the working parts
in the right places; no disease and a lookable face.

Then I began to simply see
They all had accomplished more than me.

I found my handicap was harder to trace, and it was more severe.
I found I lacked their faith and favored my fear.

I can now plainly see all that time I was laughing at me.
You know, it's not as funny now as it used to be.

Strangers

When meeting a stranger, I would rather make myself known.
Who knows what relationship may be born?

Even if it's just a simple hello
To greet that valuable fellow.
Why would I say
Something to ruin their very own day?
I may say something nice
And add a little spice
To that day of theirs.

Why see danger
In the meeting of a stranger?
Rather, see the good they surely have.
Remember you are the feared stranger to them and you surely know of all the good you possess. Just be fair,
For they also have overwhelming goodness to share.

What harm can come?
Maybe we'll share a few laughs and have a bit of fun.
It's just a meeting of two fellow strangers in a world that has too many strangers that could benefit from two less.

Money

Money will buy anything we can make,
But it alone cannot pay for a human mistake.

Money is sweet, but its taste will turn sour
If you live for it hour after hour.

Many see glory in the money they hoard, but what good will it do?
For remember, there's no taking it with you.

Money has its distinct place among our honored human race,
But too many become sick by its ungodly taste.

They lose care of what can be lost
If they allow money to be their sole boss.

There are too many different things given to do
Besides letting money make a fool out of you.

"Basic War"

They're fighting in the desert. They're fighting in the sky. They're fighting in the jungle to see if they can get the other man to die.

Say, leaders of the world, I see you're trying to solve your problems with war once again.
Do you really think that anyone will ever win?

You may claim victory and be happy with your spoils,
But how long will it be before you attack different soils?

I'm just wondering how long it will be, before you start shooting your bullets at me.
I'm just trying to live my life, praying to be free.
For some reason you think that's not to be.

I kind of feel it's just those at the top
Who never give war a chance to stop.
It's us at the bottom who have to go and solve their problems, and we do it well.
We go through hell
So they will know who was right.
We do it through a massacring fight.

I can see war has its glory
To a proud soldier.
But when the war is gone
It haunts him a whole life long,
Burdening life's simple song.
You wounded that person in their heart, and it's not easy to tear out that war wound.

What can one say to change? All I can do is hope and pray they'll find a different way to have peace come our way.

I wish I could say, "Stop your fighting in the desert. Stop your fighting in the sky. Stop your fighting in the jungle, and let's start to live with one another."

Let us finally realize we have to learn to live with and for one another,
No matter the race, creed, or color.

Working

Work is something to be happily done.
Occasionally, I'll admit, it doesn't seem like much fun.
Reaching out and doing your part.
Knowing its rewards are always felt in your heart.
I do mine and you do yours; seems only fair.
Neglect it and someone else will have to do your share.
God only knows why some people just don't care.

Too Much and Not Enough

There's too much to learn to know it all.
Too much to see to see it all.
Too much to hear to hear it all.
Too much to taste to taste it all.
Too much to touch to touch it all.
Too much to smell to smell it all.
There are too many people to meet
To meet them all.
Too much to care for to care for them all.
Just too much to do to do it all.

There's not enough food to feed them all.
Not enough clothes to clothe them all.
Not enough medicine to cure them all.
Not enough work to employ them all.
Not enough freedom to free them all.
There's not enough love to love them all.

There's too much, and there's too little.
But we can try to get more of the not-enoughs
To show them there is really more than enough!

Helping

"**H**elp," I heard the voice cry.
 Everyone looked—but I.
"**L**et her be," I began to plead—but more
 Persuasion was required of me.
 Invisible courage came to my aid.
 Nothing was impossible; we were saved.
 Great God, I never knew I was brave.

What I've Learned So Far

The Journey

The journey is infinite. The knowledge remains the same—
Just a change in our existence, living and learning on a different plane.

Each step of our journey is highly unique.
Then we realize there is still more of which to seek.

So, away we go to learn what we need to know.
It is in the universe where all questions are born.
It is in the universe where all answers are known.

How many questions have to arise before we realize
The answer is God, Master of all the stars in the skies?

The journey is infinite. The knowledge will always remain the same—
Just seeking to join God—this is our journey's aim.

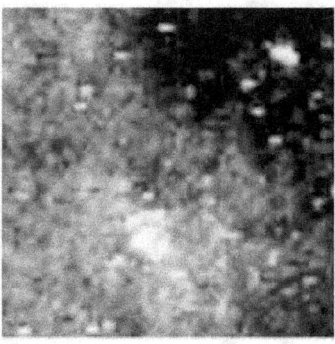

Faith and Doubt

Shadows of doubt enter the mind
To hide the light that wants to shine.

The light is faith. The shadow is doubt.
Which one can you always live without?

Encouragement

Without encouragement, the brightest star would never dare to light.
It would always feel it was no more than part of the darkness of the night.

This I Know

Visions

Looking up at the stars in all their glory,
I understand they are only part of the
universe's story.

Then, with a turn of my head, I see a simple tree
And its glory also fascinates me.

No matter how far or how close you may look,
Each miraculous part is simply a story in God's
master book.

A Drop of Love

You can open a heart with a drop of love, a drop of love
. . . a drop of love.
Oh, you can open a heart with a drop of love.
Don't you agree
Every heart needs one drop to be free?

I pray to our Father in heaven's skies to let it shower for one simple hour, a rain of love.
Let every heart catch one tiny drop.
Then all our hate will finally stop.
All it takes is one tiny drop from the rain of love
Which is blessed by God above.

An empty heart is like an empty cup.
Let's reach out and fill it up.
Fill it with a drop of friendship to let it know
Your relationship will grow.
A drop of respect shows your consideration;
A drop of kindness shows it is given free;
A drop of honesty is still the best policy;
A drop of faith to regain its pleasing taste.
A drop of courage to steer from fear.
A drop of cheer shows there's still much happiness here.

But most of all, fill it with a drop of love
And then the heart will find all of the above.

Let's reach out and, at least, try to understand
some of those small problems that hold down every
good person.
Give a drop of whatever type of love you've got
And maybe you'll help out more than you would
have thought.

You can open a heart with a drop of love, a drop of love
. . . a drop of love!

Time Left

I've got nothing but time I've been given to fully spend.
And it will be spent when I've reached the peak called
the end.

Not even a past second can be purchased or exchanged,
For past time is something that cannot be bought
or changed!

I know something has been procured
In the time that has occurred.
I pray I have no regret
In the manner it was spent.

I gladly say I have time left to freely spend.
I'll take a second glance
And give my remaining time a second chance.
There's a lot I know I can improve in the time to come.
I'll leave knowing I've left with something
positively done!

Make Ready

State of Soul

How can you ever know
The present state of your eternal soul?

I feel I will never know how I stand
Until I am departed from this land.

I rest assured I am going to go
And judgment will be made upon my soul.

This is why I should be prepared for judgment before I go.
All that will live on is my eternal soul.

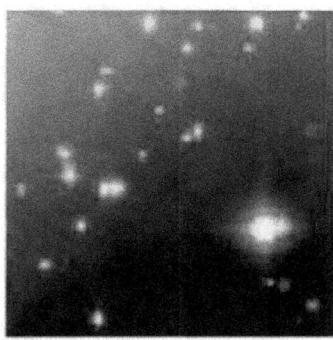

www.ingramcontent.com/pod-product-compliance
Lightning Source LLC
Chambersburg PA
CBHW072137070526
44585CB00016B/1716